Life Skills

Writing a Letter

by Emma Huddleston

FOCUS READERS

PIONEER

www.focusreaders.com

Focus Readers is distributed by North Star Editions:
sales@northstareditions.com | 888-417-0195

Produced for Focus Readers by Red Line Editorial.

Photographs ©: Shutterstock Images, cover, 1, 8, 12, 16; iStockphoto, 4, 7, 11, 15, 21; Red Line Editorial, 19

Library of Congress Cataloging-in-Publication Data
Names: Huddleston, Emma, author.
Title: Writing a letter / by Emma Huddleston.
Description: Lake Elmo, MN : Focus Readers, [2021] | Series: Life skills | Includes index. | Audience: Grades 2-3
Identifiers: LCCN 2020004743 (print) | LCCN 2020004744 (ebook) | ISBN 9781644933480 (hardcover) | ISBN 9781644934241 (paperback) | ISBN 9781644935767 (pdf) | ISBN 9781644935002 (ebook)
Subjects: LCSH: Letter writing--Juvenile literature. | English language--Composition and exercises--Juvenile literature.
Classification: LCC PE1483 .H83 2021 (print) | LCC PE1483 (ebook) | DDC 808.6--dc23
LC record available at https://lccn.loc.gov/2020004743
LC ebook record available at https://lccn.loc.gov/2020004744

Printed in the United States of America
Mankato, MN
082020

About the Author

Emma Huddleston lives in the Twin Cities with her husband. She loves writing letters to her Papa and Grandma. Emma enjoys writing children's books and reading, too.

Table of Contents

Chapter 1

The Purpose of a Letter

Family and friends send letters to one another. People often write letters for special events. They may send birthday cards. Or they may send holiday cards.

Letters help people in different places **communicate**. People write letters for many reasons. Letters take time and effort to write. So, receiving a letter can make someone feel special.

Fun Fact

The US Postal Service handles more than 187 million letters and packages every day.

Dear Mom

Chapter 2

The Beginning

The beginning of a letter has a greeting. Greetings are **polite** ways to begin talking or writing to someone. Common greetings are “Dear” or “Hello.”

The beginning of a letter also includes the name of the person you're writing to. Sometimes people add **titles** as well. Titles include "Grandma," "Uncle," "Mr.," or "Mrs." Adding a title shows **respect**.

Fun Fact

When writing a friend, you can just use his or her first name.

GRANDMA

Chapter 3

The Middle

The middle part of a letter is called the body. It is the longest part. In the body, people give their reason for writing.

People can write about their lives. They can also ask questions. People who receive letters will think about the questions. They can write back and answer the questions.

Fun Fact

Asking "How are you?" right away shows you care about the person you're writing to.

Chapter 4

The End

People use closings to end their letters. Common closings are "Love" or "See you soon." Then people sign their names.

People put letters in **envelopes**. The sender's full name and **address** go in the top-left corner of the envelope. The receiver's full name and address go in the center. A **stamp** goes in the top-right corner. The stamp pays for the letter to be sent.

Parts of a Letter

Hi Jerome, — **greeting**

How are you doing? I've been busy with basketball practice. My mom also wants me to start taking piano lessons. — **body**

See you at camp next week! — **closing**

Max — **signature**

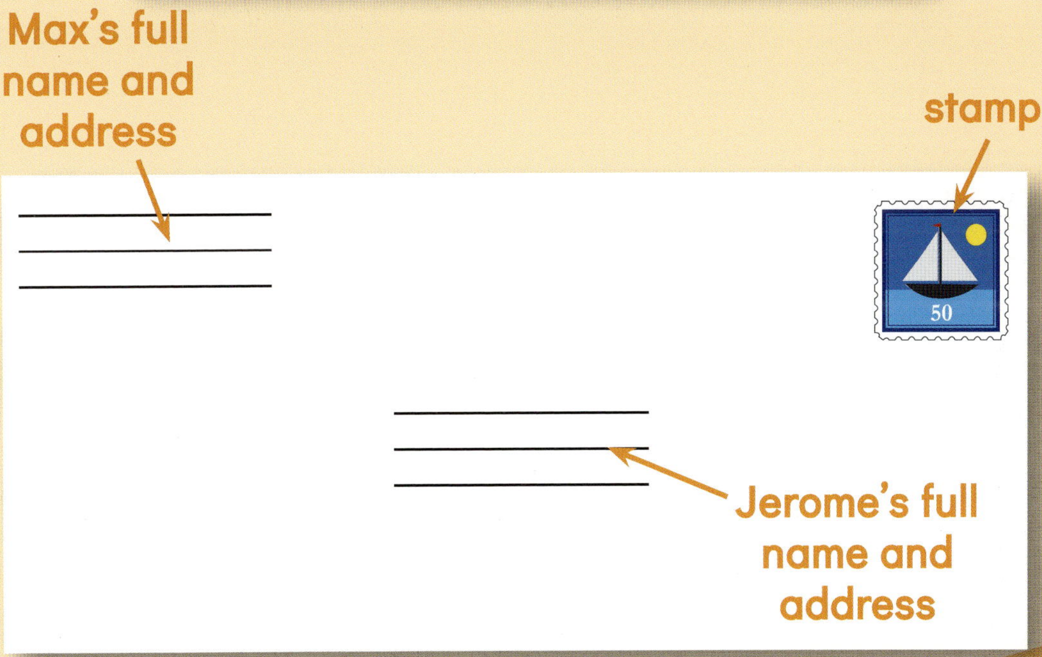

Try It Out!

Write a Letter

There are many kinds of letters. Choose one and write it.

1. Write a thank-you letter. Thank someone for his or her kind actions.
2. Write a letter to say you're sorry. You could make someone feel better.
3. Write a letter to learn about someone. What do you want to know about him or her?

Happy
Mother's
Day!

FOCUS ON

Writing a Letter

Write your answers on a separate piece of paper.

1. Write a sentence giving the main ideas of Chapter 1.
2. Do you prefer writing letters or receiving letters? Why?
3. Why do you need to put a stamp on an envelope?
   A. The stamp pays for the letter to be sent.
   B. The stamp explains why you are writing.
   C. The stamp gives the greeting.
4. Why might people write letters instead of talking in person?
   A. People might not have stamps.
   B. People might not know what to say.
   C. People might be in different places.

Answer key on page 24.

Glossary

address
A place where a person lives.

communicate
To share ideas or news with another person.

envelopes
Paper containers that letters are put into.

polite
Showing good manners.

respect
Good feelings for someone.

stamp
A sticker that shows a letter has been paid for.

titles
Words that go before people's names.

To Learn More

BOOKS

Kenan, Tessa. *Hooray for Mail Carriers!* Minneapolis: Lerner Publications, 2018.

Murray, Julie. *Mail Carriers.* Minneapolis: Abdo Publishing, 2016.

NOTE TO EDUCATORS

Visit **www.focusreaders.com** to find lesson plans, activities, links, and other resources related to this title.

Index

Answer Key: 1. Answers will vary; **2.** Answers will vary; **3.** A; **4.** C